DATE DUE

NOV _ 8			

Demco, Inc. 38-293

D1088642

GIVE PROBABILITY A CHANCE!

by Thomas K. and Heather Adamson

Consultant:
Tamara Olson, Associate Professor
Department of Mathematical Sciences
Michigan Technological University

CAPSTONE PRESS
a capstone imprint

A+ Books are published by Capstone Press,
1710 Roe Crest Drive, North Mankato, Minnesota 56003.
www.capstonepub.com

Library of Congress Cataloging-in-Publication Data
Cataloging-in-publication information is on file with the Library of Congress.
ISBN 978-1-4296-7558-1 (hardcover)
ISBN 978-1-4296-7859-9 (paperback)

Credits

Kristen Mohn, editor; Gene Bentdahl, designer; Svetlana Zhurkin, media researcher; Laura Manthe,
production specialist; Sarah Schuette, photo stylist; Marcy Morin, studio scheduler

Photo Credits

All photos by Capstone Studio/Karon Dubke except: Dreamstime/Ruzanna Arutyunyan, 7 (inset)

Note to Parents, Teachers, and Librarians

This Fun with Numbers book uses photos of everyday objects in a nonfiction format to introduce
the concept of chance and probability, including making educated guesses based on known facts
and understanding degrees of likelihood. *Give Probability a Chance!* is designed to be read aloud
to a pre-reader or to be read independently by an early reader. The book encourages further
learning by including the following sections: Table of Contents, Taking It Further, Read More, and
Internet Sites. Early readers may need assistance using these features.

Printed in the United States of America in North Mankato, Minnesota.
102011   006405CGS12

TABLE of CONTENTS

What Is Probability?

It's Mia's birthday. Her party was going to be outside, but the weather reporter said there is a chance of rain. That means maybe it will rain and maybe it will not.

We use probability to describe which things are more likely or less likely to happen. Sometimes things are certain, like day and night. Sometimes things are impossible, like getting younger instead of older. But possible things may or may not happen. We have to use clues to make a guess. That's probability!

Watch for these words in the book:

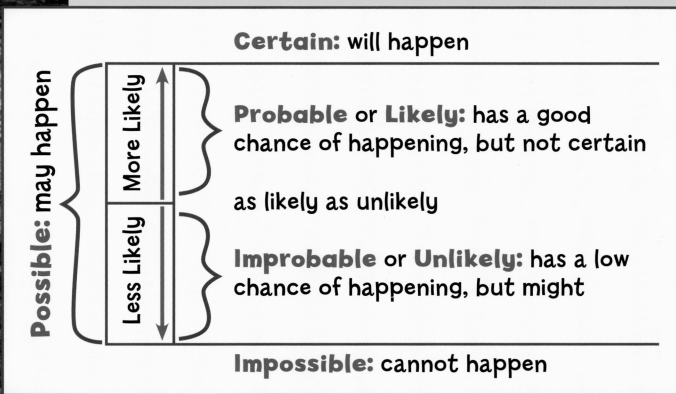

Possible: may happen

More Likely / Less Likely

Certain: will happen

Probable or **Likely:** has a good chance of happening, but not certain

as likely as unlikely

Improbable or **Unlikely:** has a low chance of happening, but might

Impossible: cannot happen

Mia looks for the mail while she waits for her friends to arrive. She is certain that a mail carrier will bring the mail today. It's possible that he will deliver a birthday gift for her.

It's party time, and there's no rain yet. At the park, Ken and Rico are at the top of the yellow slide. Who will come down first? It's equally likely that it will be either of them. The chances are the same.

But it's **least likely** for Mia to come down the slide first. She's waiting her turn.

Rico was first!

Making Good Guesses

Here come some dark clouds!
It might rain soon, so the
kids go inside for treats
and games.

Ken reaches into a bag that has all red candies.
He is certain to pull out a red candy.

What if Mia puts one green
candy in his bag?

Without looking, it is improbable that Ken would
pick the green candy out of all those red ones,
but it is possible.

Put the blindfold on, Mia! Which color tail is she more likely to pick?

Mia is more likely to pick a tail with a red ribbon, because there are three of those. There are only two tails with blue ribbons, so there is less chance of choosing that color.

Is it **likely** or **unlikely** that Mia will put the tail on the right spot on the donkey?

No peeking!

What Are the Chances?

Look at this game spinner. There is an equal chance of landing on any of the four colors. What's the chance of landing on blue?

Because blue is one of four equally likely outcomes, we say that the chances are one-in-four, or 1/4.

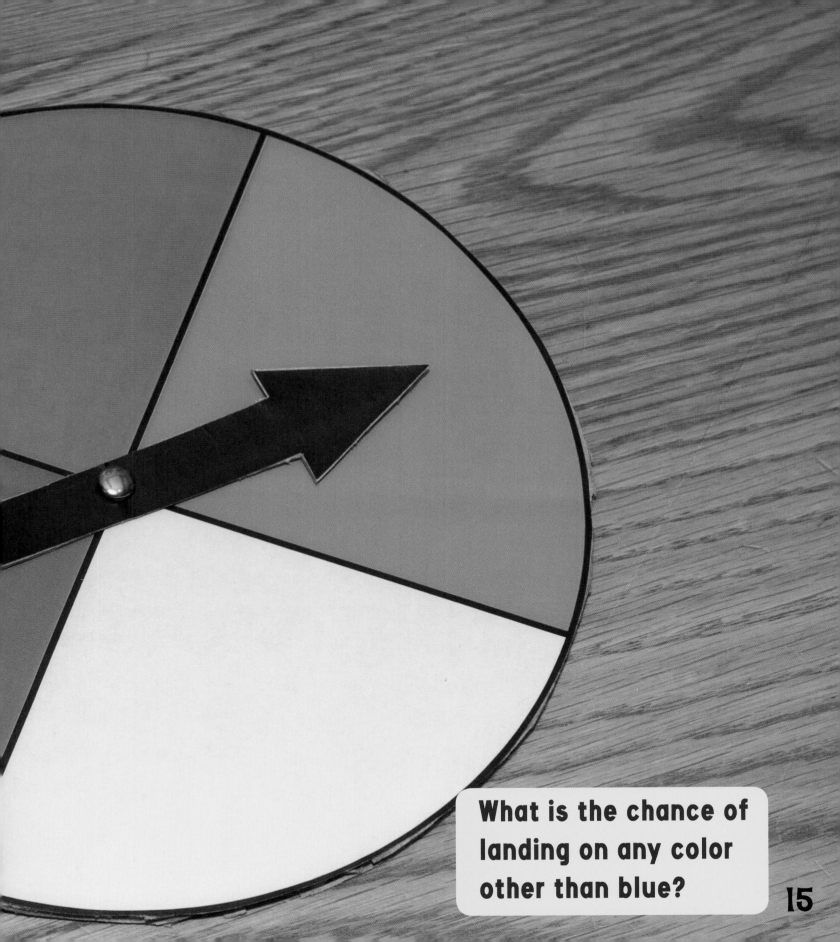

What is the chance of landing on any color other than blue?

15

Here's a spinner with four colors plus "Lose a Turn." Luckily, the spinner is more likely to land on a color space than on "Lose a Turn." Can you see why?

All together, 8 spins landed on colors. Only 2 spins landed on "Lose a Turn."

Who wants to play target toss? The target has three scoring areas. The middle is worth the most points. But it's the smallest. The outside ring is worth the fewest points. It's the largest area to hit.

It's **more probable** for the beanbags to land on the larger areas. The small bull's-eye is **less probable**.

19

Rico's on a roll! He got doubles twice in a row! Rolling doubles is unlikely but possible. He was very lucky. If Rico and Mia each roll the dice again, who is more likely to get doubles?

The chances are the same for everybody on each roll. It doesn't matter what was rolled the last time.

Let's test this with 10 more rolls. Rico rolled doubles one more time!

1	3	5
2	1	2
3	4	5
4	6	4
5	2	3
6	3	6
7	1	4
8	5	2
9	4	2
10	6	6

Rico's Rolls

Missy the Magician puts a red, a blue, and an orange scarf in her hat. She reaches in to pull one out. What is the chance that it will be the red one?

There are three colors. One of them is red. So the chances are one-in-three (1/3). The chances are the same for orange or blue too.

When she pulls the scarves out, they're all tied together.
You didn't guess that, did you? It's magic!

Using Clues

A probability guess depends on the information you have.

At the party there are two cupcake choices—chocolate and vanilla.

24

If you know that Mia and her friends like chocolate more than vanilla, which flavor would be likely to run out first?

There are also two drink choices at the party—five each of apple juice and lemonade. But you can't tell which is which.

Ken wants lemonade. His chances are one-in-two (1/2). He pulls out an apple juice first. Try again, Ken!

If he sets the apple juice aside and chooses again, which flavor is he more likely to get this time?

Probability isn't for sure. It helps you make a good guess.

The weather reporter thought it would probably rain today. Mia is glad his guess was wrong!

CHECK YOUR PROBABILITY GUESSES

Page 13:
It looks like Mia is unlikely to pin the tail on the donkey correctly. She seems likely to pin it on his head!

Pages 14-15:
The chance of landing on any other color other than blue is three-in-four (3/4).

Pages 16-17:
There are four colors and one Lose-a-Turn space on the spinner. That's a four-in-five chance of landing on a color, and a one-in-five chance of landing on Lose-a-Turn. So you're more likely to land on a color.

Pages 24-25:
If more kids like chocolate, that flavor is likely to run out first. But some kids might decide to try vanilla today, so it's not certain!

Page 27:
Ken's chances of getting lemonade are better this time, because there are still five of those, and only four apple juices left. His chance is now five-in-nine (5/9).

TAKING IT FURTHER

If there were 10 blue balls in a bag and no other colors, what would your chances be of pulling a blue ball out of the bag? Ten-in-ten (10/10). That's definite. What if you add one red ball to the 10 blue ones? How likely is it that you will pull out the red one?

When you flip a coin, there are only two choices of how it will land—heads or tails. The chances are 1/2. Flip a coin 10 times. How many times does it come up heads and how many tails? Now try 50 flips. Are your results what you expected?

Try watching a weather report like Mia did before her party. Listen for words like chance, likely, possible, and probable. Keep track of the weather and see what happens.

GLOSSARY

certain—will happen

chance—the possibility of something happening

doubles—two of the same

equal—the same as something else in size, number, or value

impossible—cannot happen

improbable—has a low chance of happening

outcome—result

possible—may happen

probability—how likely or unlikely it is for something to happen

probable—has a good chance of happening

READ MORE

Aboff, Marcie. *Pigs, Cows, and Probability*. Data Mania. Mankato, Minn.: Capstone, 2011.

Einhorn, Edward. *A Very Improbable Story*. Watertown, Mass.: Charlesbridge, 2008.

Leedy, Loreen. *It's Probably Penny*. New York: H. Holt, 2007.

INTERNET SITES

FactHound offers a safe, fun way to find Internet sites related to this book. All of the sites on FactHound have been researched by our staff.

Here's all you do:

Visit *www.facthound.com*

Type in this code: 9781429675581

Super-cool stuff!

Check out projects, games and lots more at
www.capstonekids.com